Her Album

Aaliyah Whitley

Presentation by *BookLeaf Publishing*

Web: www.bookleafpub.com

E-mail: info@bookleafpub.com

ISBN: 9789395026697

First edition 2022

DEDICATION

I would like to dedicate this book to those that understand the melody of what this reality sounds and feels like just as much as I can.

ACKNOWLEDGEMENT

I would like to acknowledge and thank Book Leaf Publishing for being apart of this amazing journey with me. Thank you for making my purpose effective.

PREFACE

The writing of this book brought out the feelings I knew most people wouldn't really understand because of the experiences I have faced and continue to face to some extent at an age that someone would have something going for themselves so it's almost seldom to most people. It came about within the most darkest and loneliest times of my life when those I wanted and needed the most we're no longer able to play a purpose in my life anymore because of the plans God had for me and my life. From public school being the norm for me most of my life to homeschool being the rest of my school experience, that's when everything took a turn for the bitter and the sweet. From there I had no choice but to be strong after having to start from square one again. I had to put away the clowning that got me through elementary and middle school, along with my immature selfishness of what I wanted my life to look like and take in what I dished out when it came to who I use to be to get out of the place I wanted to run from for so long and that was isolation . It would follow me everywhere I went and no Matter where I would escape there it was . And I finally stopped running from it when it met me at the

the weakest point of my life, that involved depression and heartbreak. From there I knew it was serious and I knew that something had to give because I would not be able to handle separating myself from the people and things I was so attached to. from there I knew I was isolated because of the preparation for the purpose I have here, and all of a sudden all of the feelings I conjured up within my poems became the Album of this season in my life.

Unworthy

I am feeling unworthy,
Not because I am not worthy
But because I am.

Unworthiness has stabbed
My veins and so it bleeds.
The errors of me it reads.

My failures, mistakes, and flaws
Flare up my destruction.
It tore me down so I am
In need of construction.

Unworthy.
Because my love is unworthy
To my own service, my worth
Is worthy when people can attest.

Mind games

And there the games began...
1:00 a.m.
you were thrown in the ocean.

You try not to think about how there is a chance
you could drown.

If you feel lust or heartbreak,
If you act upon it…you…drown.
What is it that will keep you from drowning?

All I want is for the ocean
To wash out the pain…
Not to take my whole life.

The memories lifespan
Needs to be taken…
Yet it sucks my energy up under
Me like a leech.

"It's okay"

Stop telling me it's going to be ok.
Stop telling me what Direction to go
And which way.

If you woke up just to breathe
And not to live,
Most of you would cry and hate the
Reason of each day.

People speaking on me
But I can't press them, because
You have to be the families
Good girl so you don't stress them.

Faking the happy role with my
Head held high and my heart down low,
Constantly fighting to stay away
From the wrong road,
But if I go then everybody will talk and know.

I don't know what is next but
Don't talk to me like my problem is small.
If you walked in my shoes
The position I'm in would be tall.

Lust

When I feel you lust,
I feel my heart being crushed
And this rough feeling
Of a deceitful rush.

Intoxicating the world
With this lie,
That bringing lust into a relationship
Is where it should fly.

Why do we trust your feelings,
When you are
The reason for a spirits killing
Or for a broken relationship that gets no healing.

It's okay because you won't get away,
I will expose the reality
And pray God gives us a greater way.

Traumas corner

Save me lord save me,
Because evil is trying to enslave me.
My back is against the wall
As the creator of evil caves me.

He has fought to make me
Who he is, a heartless soul with
No hope.
I don't see the damage on my neck,
But I can feel the invisible rope.

He has shaped me into
My traumatic reflections,
So every time I feel comfort
It feels suspicious so I reject it.

And as I cry for peace,
And you try to save me
My natural instinct is to neglect it.

The only hope I have is to be
Still and wait on you God,
Knowing that your my only refuge…

In four walls stranded.

Traumas corner II

This void...
This void is so dark and quiet
Yet so painful and loud.

This void makes me distant,
It excludes me from the crowd.
I feel empty here and physically bound.

Resilience is my cover up
But my healing is my only get
Getaway.

I'm fighting for a good future
But my hands are tired,
Completion is my desire.

I just want to make it home.

Happiness

I'm feeling alive again,
In my heart I'm feeling the thrive within.
With happiness taking it's part

I'm feeling the art within.
My heart changed to
Colorful art.

Can't break

There are times
Of no understanding,
There are times of flying
But yet no right landing .

There are times when
You wake up yet you feel blind,
Because you didn't realize the mercy
God gave you to wake up another time .

You feel broken
So you break, you got taken
Advantage of so you take.

You got looked down on
So now you hate,
So now all the wrong decisions
You choose to make.

Controlled by society

In this world I'm an
Alien walking around, with the
Darkest of eyes staring me down.

As if my skin is invisible
And my life shows in spirit outwardly.
I am the complexion of a light
No one has ever seen

Like a color in heaven
You've never seen.
I am an outcast in humankind.

In my eyes people walk around
With this mark on the
Top of their heads
That says "controlled by society"

And from what I've seen, there
We're people in big varieties.

Divine direction

We lose what we want
For what we need.
But we never get what we need

Because what we want,
We continue to chase after.

What we want can be the
Reason we never get what we
Need which leaves us with nothing
Left,

So then life becomes a theft.
Hope isn't always around when you
Only hear silence around you.

When you compromise who
You are for others...
Your no longer inside of your body...
Your just a puppet.

Radiant spirit

As the sun shines with
My feet walking on the side walk
Colored in beige.

My spirit is as radiant
As the sun, to where the
Sun becomes the moon.

As God protects me, I feel
Like I have entered a
Castle because I am royalty.

I have so many creative layers
To myself, my persona is like
A quiet museum.

Self / ish

Are you afraid of you?
Is it fear of what you can't do?

You get so impatient you
Have a picture perfect
Point to prove.

Present

I figured it out beloved
I'm a gift,
Which causes me to be in this box.

My Christmas has not yet
Come.
I am not allowed to be presented
At the moment.

I continue to unwrap
Myself prolonging my own time.
Oh box, oh box…let
Me blossom.

God help me sit still.

Dream girl

My appearance is silence
But my spirit screams,
Within my mind there are so
Many soon to come dreams.

My wings to soar are written
On paper,
I am like a bird and a butterfly
With so many beautiful colors
For the people around me to witness.

I am the shadow of healing,
I am a women that gives a contagious
Mellow feeling.

I am like the scent of a hand picked
Rose, because just like
It, I've grown from the dirt.

I am deeper than a walk in the
Park, I am a walk on
The beach where the sound of peace
Never ends.

I am never the girl you see with

Your eyes open, I am the woman
You want with your eyes closed.
Your dream girl.

Her discernment

I'm a woman.
I'm a woman walking on
Her own two feet.

I got wings on my
Back but i'm on earth
So imma keep it sweet.
I'm on a planet where people swim

In kitty pools and
Claim they're deep
While they're working with
The wolves and claim that they're sheep.

I'm on the sea
With Peter and Jesus, I'm
On a mission so when
you see me, you see us.

Her discernment II

I stay down on
My knees for God to
Free my generation

But everybody's
So busy playing
Halloween with Satan.

It's like signing
Your life away to the
Music industry and

Now your soul is taken.
Getting tricked you get a treat
For that, but I can see

Through that,
You know me by the fruits
So spoiled fruits I can't eat from that.

Higher

I have found myself,
I have found "I" within a spirit, a holy one
Floating within me, it feels
Like ocean waves.
It is as silent as a stillness,
It's my company so
Much, that if I don't have it
I could be around another
Physical being and somehow feel like
There is nobody in the room.
It is my thirst, that somehow not
Enough water out of this whole
Entire world could possibly quench my
Thirst.
It flies within me like a butterfly,
That there is no such man that
Could insert millions of butterflies
Within my stomach to amount to
The one butterfly the Holy Spirit
Gives.
With it within me I am finally
Completed, that nothing else
is nearly needed.
I fly,I fly, we fly.
Let's explore what's higher

Than the sky.

In and out

Oh God, what breath am I
Breathing without being obedient
Unto your word?

It's thought of the breath
Physically that I seem
To grasp.

Why can't I spiritually breath ?
I'm in a spiritual coma where
My mind debates to be spiritually
Dead or alive.

I'm in a physical dream
For the spiritual, to make this
Choice for the results.
My breath is currently in between,

I pass away but I come back
Once again.
I would never ask to pull the
Plug on my spiritual oxygen...

God help me
Push for my spiritual life.

God's hand

I will continue to write
until God wants me to stop.
I will continue to believe that
I'm under his wing and he's on top.

God I need your hand,
I need you to help me take a stand
Against my doubts.

God make me a light for the blinded
Such as myself.
Help me be true to what you
Have put inside me.

Give my mind a new free
Space, take the messed up
pieces of the broken vase,
Help me never give up on my
Faith

But help me give all that it takes.

The alpha poet

As I think about the
Poetic words of Jesus,
I feel the compatibility that the
Creator and I have.

He has created in me a heart
Filled with unexplainable
Messages he has given unto
Me to explain to the best of my
God given gift.

The words of God are artistic
Truth. His words are
So advanced, the worlds most
Accelerated poetic couldn't outdo it.

The ending

In the ending of
Which this earth is going,
There is a pause of which way to go
As I take my next steps
Into the new phase
Of living.
I can inwardly
See everything around
Us disappear slowly yet so quickly.

The changes
Of life that my generation
Will discover will be heavenly things.
Coming into that reality
Is a change beyond measures that the
Human body
Can not even mentally
Understand because this gravity
Of life is all we can take in.